FOUND WORDS

Edward E. Valentine

Found Words © 2007 by Edward E. Valentine
Front Cover Image © 2007 by Edward E. Valentine
Photo of Poet © 2007 by Kevin L. Donihe

Edward E. Valentine, Publisher,
Mt. Carmel, TN (USA)

Printed in the United States of America

Editing: Kevin L. Donihe
Interior Layout/Cover Design: Kevin L. Donihe

All rights reserved, including the right to reproduce this book or portions thereof in any form whatsoever except as provided by U.S. Copyright Law.

ISBN: 978-0-6151-4399-6

*Dedicated to Kevin L. Donihe
for making this possible.*

CONTENTS:

Morning
My Heart
Found Words
Falling Leaves
Raindrops
Summer's Dream Amongst the Stars
That I Am
Right or Wrong
Flesh of Beauty
Two Hearts
Mingled
Hidden
One Day
Summers Past
Flower in the Stream
The Beginning
Touching
Dream
The Feather
In July
Fly Byes
The Sea
This Season
Placed
A Heart
Beams of Moonlight
Blank Paper
Forevermore
Trip and Fall
Winds of Time
The Shadow Moves
A Short Time

Covers All
Wild Side
Beyond the Mountain
To Come
My Way
Lost!
Renewed
Beyond Earth and Sky
Captured Mind
In the Realm of Things
Another Life
I Will
Blessed
Another Place and Time
To Stay
Just I
Close As
Steps
Your Breath
His Voice
Willing
Without End
Touching Life
Tears of Salvation
Ever Wondered?
At Twlight
Unbounded Love
Blue-Eyed Tears
To Comprehend
There is No Excuse
The Joy of a Day
To Keep
Today
Words of Destiny

FOUND WORDS

INTRODUCTION:

At the age of 10—being a military kid and growing up during the Viet Nam period in the land of 'guess what'—I realized how poetry had the power to release inner emotions. Over the years, I wrote more and more until I had enough to fill a collection. Now that it's published, I consider FOUND WORDS another step in my life taken.

Finally, I'd like to thank everyone who takes the time to read this book. I hope it speaks to all who will listen.

—Edward E. Valentine
genevalentine59@msn.com
MySpace: myspace.com/genevalentine

May 26, 2007

Morning

I arise with the sun;
bird songs echo in my room.
Dawn drifts away
with the smell of morning flowers.
Step forward into this day;
make ready for tomorrow
so the Son can rise again
and breathe new life into me.

My Heart

In my heart, search for the words
to put on this page.
Thoughts of mine, or of another time,
or of a dream, opening my heart,
leading me into your hands.
This is my fate,
and here I will find the reason.

Found Words

On cloudless days and moonlit nights,
cross the winds of time on shifting sand,
guided by stars that burn heavenly blue
beyond shadowed mountain peaks.

My destination is known in the twinkling
of life's comings and goings
as a falling star streaks across the sky
and fades with my last drop of water.

I sleep to dream under cliff shadows
and, upon awakening,
bathe in morning dew.

After two days of scorching heat,
eating the flesh and drinking the blood of the wild,
rain stirs the dust at my feet,
removing my tears

and filling me with new found words.

Falling Leaves

Yellow with a touch of orange and green,
wafting in the wind,
drifting into clouds
—the shifting current tests their limits.

Hold onto the flow of life.

On Blue Mountain, rain turns to sleet
as a cold wind blows,
changing time to begin
where everything ends

in the branches of life.

Raindrops

The moon rises with the shifting winds,
changing colors across the horizon;
the sun hides behind clouds.

Lightning flashes across the night,
revealing crouching shadows
as tears of angels fall from the sky

and awaken in raindrops.

Summer's Dream Amongst the Stars

Sunlight plays in my hair
as shadows move across my eyes.
In this field I lay
in the peace of my Maker.

*This was all given to me
to enjoy while others seek.
Now you can see, too.
A mind of dreams
has been given to you
by His blood, flowing in the stream.*

*Everyday, the wind blows like breath,
but even flowers breathe their last,
and, in a twinkling of an eye,
I'm in the heavens of eternity.*

Water gleams as warm winds blow
through a golden field
with blooms of many colors.
I live amongst them all in God's hands
—He who keeps me amongst the stars.

That I Am

Envision winds, sail across skies,
enter times of dream and vision
as fantasy and reality mix.
Physical desires, deep passion,
conciseness—find these elements,
your soul trapped in life and death.
Spirits wander like the winds,
their temples against the horizon.
Shadows call for the sun to rise,
revealing light, the truth in all:
One spirit.

Right or Wrong

Right or wrong, left or right?
Half full or half empty are the thoughts of mankind.
A pinhole at the bottom of the glass
drips a thousand drops.
Bottomless darkness leaks;
see the light behind it.
Thoughts fall into the half empty/full glass;
words of mankind
move steps left or right;
his creation, right or wrong,
fills the glass.

Flesh of Beauty

With the steam and whistle blowing,
our moods come together on this train
as I get closer for a touch
of your warm flesh of beauty.

My timeless desire
gleams of sunsets and rainbows
found in the evening sky.

Dreams abound.

Reality enters
through the windows
of your soul.

Two Hearts

It takes two wings, for without both
no wind, no power, will allow you to fly.
Together, we lift each other in romance,
and this takes two hearts, beating together
with sweet and pleasant desire.

Your eyes and smile bring joy to my heart.
I hope these roses bring joy to yours.
May your days bloom with the pleasure
your smile brings me.

The Creator created you, then the rose.

Mingled

In time, desire turns to love.
We feel the need to be wanted,
to be held in serenity
while searching for
fulfillment in life.
Blinded, we stumble and fall
only to rise to a cause
—our souls mingling
in passion and desire,
revealing awareness.

Hidden

See the splendor in this morning;
smell the flowers covered in dew.
Find hidden passions while dreaming
dreams of yesterday
in the mist of a morning reborn.
The flowers are awakening,
dressed in their best to attract the bee and me.
He finds his honey, too.

One Day

My eyes see the wonder in it all,
the anguish, suffering, and pain.
Days go by in a twinkling;
memories of our past times,
of crying tears
as fisted hands hold onto life
and she speaks to yesterdays.

No matter how bad things get
there's some good in this;
she can still find a smile
to take their place.

The Blessings of God
will take *her* place.

I see the wonder;
there's always time for a smile.
Even in the worst of times
God's grace reveals
my mother's love.

Summers Past

Yesterday's memories
gleam through windows past.
Summer days of pure love,
walk their paths
to the end. Hold on;
hearts reveal the wisdom of ages.

Share smiling faces daily,
life with a grin
and happiness found in small places.
Remember
what comes and goes
and drift slowly to sleep,
again and again
—dreaming of summers past.

Flower in the Stream

Moon shadows reflect on the water
just before nightfall.

Dreams of yesterday
become dreams of today.

Find the flow of life
beyond mountains and dreams

… a flower in the stream.

The Beginning

As a child, I cast a flower upon the water
with visions of my Lord reaching out,
His hands picking up the flower
as The Spirit of God ran through my heart.
His glow was like none I had ever seen.
My Holy Father awaits me;
this life I must endure.

You are the flower in My hand,
and the water of eternal life, I offer you.
My Spirit, I give to you
for I am the vine of the flower.
As I gave life to the flower, I also gave it to you.
The water's flow is My blood.
Your sins, I washed away;
your faith has saved you.

Memories He gave me, I now share with you.
His will be done, not mine.
So I now flow in His blood
and in His hands I am
forever in Eternity.
He came to you, with your faith given.
Now cast another flower His way:
The Beginning.

Touching

The light of life reflects
along the surface of land and sea.
Look to the beauty of the skies;
stir in wonder; touch my soul.

To the Creator of man
and to the stars above
I offer humble words,
memories never forgotten,
dreams of yesterday
and figments of the mind.

Tomorrow begins a new life
when our souls touch the glory in Him,
knocking at the door to your heart,
touching that which is you.

Dream

Footsteps echo things to come
as breathless passions follow stars,
enrapturing all who see.
Wonders will come and go
as sunlight brings rainbows
through falling snow,
paints the cloudy evening sky,
and tops great canyon cliffs
to the sound of waterfalls
below which two lovers dream.

The Feather

The feather is part of the eagle as he flies.
At all times
they are inseparable.
So take care the feather
and the feather will take care of you.
In times of battle and peace,
you are One; so fly together
through this life
to the end.

In July

On life's trails
sunrays gleam
behind mountains,
silhouetting
blue gray skies
and bringing satisfaction
to the mind
and peace
in the eye of the storm.

Drift into sleep,
cooled by the winds
of a squall;
find rest and comfort
amongst the shadows of time.
This day until tomorrow,
dream dreams of today
come as they may
in July.

Fly Byes

A color burst flashes by, faster than a falling star
Stopped! To stir, fixed in the air,
humming sweet joy
and partaking of dew and nectar
found in red trumpets below.
Humming wing songs float over crimson blooms
then disappear without a goodbye.
The hummingbird stopped to say a quick hello,
but, in a twinkling, his hello
flew by.

The Sea

Brimming with life,
it jumps for joy each evening.
Over it, the sun sails
into yellow and red-gold skies,
touching stars at perfect points
that dazzle with each twinkling
—life swimming a journey
guided by sun rays,
constantly moving in time
or on a summer's breeze.
Follow the stars
where the clouds cross
the sea ...

This Season

Standing on a rock
with water flowing at my feet,
seeing the sun rise above the stars
—my crown I cast at *Your* feet,
and there I lay my head.

May You bless and guide me
in a world of many colors
and dreams that seek tomorrow
while living in yesterday
in memory and routine.

Guide me, in this life of mind,
for You are the reason
I am here this season.

Placed

Reflections of snowy peaks
on blue water
guided me to new life.
I stood mesmerized,
surrounded by shadows of tall spruces
leaning fixed in the direction of the wind,
bleached timbers stacked like toothpicks
on the northern Pacific coast
and smooth stones of color,
shaped by ocean tides.
I left footprints on gray and shifting sand.

A thousand pictures I took.
Never could I justify the glory of it,
created by God
… steps in another place and time.

A Heart

The word of man moves the air;
echoes stream through the clouds to the universe,
romancing the devil, controlling the waves
found deep within the future.

Peace to all who listen.
Peace to those surrounded by the love of Christ.
Peace in the Morning Star and the Lilly of the Valley.
Peace inside the words of men
who love God.

Hear sounds of joy and enlightenment
echoing deeply within these words
as sure as the air moves
a heart to pray,
saying …

Beams of Moonlight

Through stardust shadowed
by the moon and limbs in deep forest
fall snowflakes before the heavens.
The breath of God
touches another flake.

Imagination calls to the stars.

Beams of moonlight;
man's heart.

Blank Paper

I turn the page
and, through the eyes of the spirit,
arrive wonders untold.

Imagination and eternity
come together
on blank paper.

Forevermore

Tears of life flowing within unbounded love,
stretched beyond heaven's horizontal sky;
stand in the midst of it all.
In valleys and on mountain tops flowers bloom
through the tempest of life passed.
God's revealing thoughts
paint the earth in living colors
wonderful to mankind's dreams
—today's words of tomorrow's blooms.

Your shadow moved
the Light of mankind,
uniquely driven and each given
the stroke of living color that seeps into life.
With His hands stretched out
the risen Son comes.
The four corners of the earth;
the wonder of it all.
No flower petal shadows fall from His hands;
the Lily of the Valley blooms forevermore.

Trip and Fall

Visions twinkle fast as starlight
on a dark and cold winter night
seen through a flickering glare.
Drift asleep on ocean waves
under candlelit fantasy.

Feel cool air touch your face
and awaken to the full moon
only to trip and fall
over the wonder of it all.

Went to bed for a winter's dream.
Words of time;
see what's there.
During a winter's full moon
words will come.

Thoughts and dreams of a world apart
shall never depart
men both young and old.

Winds of Time

Seasons drift with the winds of time beyond mankind.
Realities of dreams, to come.
Lives, in a summer's dust storm,
move the dust of men's ghosts
on winds of time.

Shapes of dark and gray above the horizon,
screams heard in the sound of the winds;
lost words echo past generations
just before the storm.

The Shadow Moves

Dreams come together for a short time
in heaven's place.
Through the touching
of the souls of mankind,
the Dragon's shadow moves.

A Short Time

Tennessee to Seattle, Washington we flew
over snow peaked mountains, lakes of blue.
Rivers of lifeblood streamed
above rain swollen clouds
and visions of hills and valleys
through snowflakes' white wonder seen.
Rainbows spanned darkened horizons;
Pacific winds blew clouds to the top
of Hurricane Ridge
and over the tracks and trails of mankind
—boundaries of rivers and state lines
visible for a short time.

Covers All

To those who believe
I stand at your hearts,
eternal faith
walks in unseen.

I am that I am.

I hear your prayers—
above you, in Holy Spirit
—praising My joy
in the hearts of men
who receive Me
in this House of Prayer.

All is revealed in the flow of life,
touching your souls
in the Light, living in My being,
and in the blood of the cross.
Love grants eternal life
to all who believe.

My spirit covers all.

Wild Side

In my youth
I walked amongst the streams of the wild,
surrounded by forest leaves,
misty moss and flowers,
and sounds near a waterfall's rainbow
all seen through the sun's rays.

At creek bottom, clear water shone
as rainbow trout swam the rock and boulder maze.
Then a sound lifted my eyes
to a flower glimpsed in red hair.
Beyond the rainbow she stood in morning's light
—memories of rainbows and leaves
on the wild side of my younger days.

Beyond the Mountain

Rhododendron blooms
near a lady in slippers
as limbs point the way
on this summer's day
to the valley
where my true love lives
and my heart
will always stay.

To Come

Earthquakes shake, rattle and roll,
shaping the Earth.

Leaves of yellow and red fall;
dew drops on a winter's call.

Words speak from past memories
and moments turn into years to come.

Rocks crumble to sand,
flowing into the sea of time.

Death comes with both joy and suffering;
mankind will answer *his* call

—words of divinity
found in a rainbow sky.

My Way

Reality plays with my mind
in this world between walls of concrete and steel.

I take short steps in fives-by-fifteens.
My heart looks for new memories and games to play,
blind to realities created with each step
made between these walls.

Warnings ignored, I pay the price of life
just because I had to have it
my way.

Lost!

Descriptive words are hard to find
in living art, mountains and coastlines.
Sunsets and sunrises magnify an imagination
infused with joy and majesty.

Clouds move across an ocean of evening sky
and change with every mountain peak.
I turn around in amazement,
each thought creating another then another.

Speechless, I stand,
heart touched beyond words,
here on my spot of living earth
West, on Sunset Boulevard.

Renewed

Smell aromas
carried by the breeze—
sweet honey to bees
—and awaken to a day
fully bloomed.

Find nectar gleaming,
sunrise yellow touched
by morning's glow.
Here, rose petals abound,
God's hand holding each,
the glory found within
giving to man
the path of the rose
lying at the foot
of the cross at Calvary.

The love of a rose,
a path for man
to follow from the blood,
waiting for us
to take our first step,
renewed.

Beyond Earth and Sky

The smile of an angelic face
below eyes of joy and song
makes me remember our first real kiss,
pure as the love we create
and find from above.

Experience things unimaginable
—passion without boundaries or time.
These summer dreams
beyond earth and sky
move only for you and I,

true love.

Captured Mind

What does it take to capture the mind?
The aroma of a rose or love in the air.
Forgotten dreams coming true.
Love-to-hate, feelings turning to blues.
Fast lanes and short stops.
A child's words.
New patience for living.
It takes all;
touching one's heart with songs of love
and midnight dreams of a captured mind.

In the Realm of Things

Now, in the realm of things
gather moss from the shadows of man,
covered by man and his tracks in time
on his quest to fill the loneliness
deep in his heart.

Fill it with feelings and desires,
each and every one, filling their hearts
in the realm of things, playing
near sunlit, flowing streams
and in the fields and streets of dreams
found within.

Another Life

A sign from heaven, or just thoughts of mind,
together in a passing dream across the sky,
traveling in your hand, glorying in your Creation
—a globe amongst the stars and heavens,
a gleaming jewel.

Stretching starlight before me this night
brought such thoughts to mind.
Together in this space and time,
another life I will find.

I Will

I pray God will give me the words
that I leave with you
—words from the depth of my heart.
Blessed were your mother and me
with your soul in our life,
to touch your warmth.

To God, I give my love
for my son.

To you, I leave my words
burned into your heart and soul,
whispering thunder in your ears.
Will you hear me, listen for me?

I will ...

Blessed

Words I search for deep within,
finding memories of you, my firstborn,
touched by God with each heartbeat.

So here's *my* heart, my tears,
and a few words
written with eternal love.

You're the sunrise of a new day;
a touch of dew on a morning's rose
came into my life with you,

blessed.

Another Place and Time

Tired from this long journey
of dry heat and sand
that calls up thoughts
of another place and time,
I fall deep into a believable dream
as my grandfather's words in sleep
echo out of the distant storm.

To Stay

Let me write words of joy
found in the love of God,
soul reaching
beyond any dream or song.

A life within touches me
when thunder outside
heralds an evening rainbow sky.

Standing in the fall breeze,
eyes closed,
the spirit glows within
bringing joy and peace
—and here I want to stay.

Just I

Oh this is a night for love, dear.
Though we are many miles apart,
nevertheless, over these blue green waters,
Beloved, I send you my heart.
The moon and the stars
will carry it and place it in your hands
for you to keep until I return,
home again from foreign lands.
So, if a moonbeam kisses you,
or a star should blink in the night,
It is I, my love, just I.

Such are the words from my heart,
carried from the heavens above,
to be given to my one true love.

Close As

Valentine to heart.
Petal to flower.
Day to sunrise.
First breath of a child.
A friend in need.
A crown to a queen or king.
Light to morning.
Sweetness to honey.
Forever to eternity.
The love in your heart,
close as the breath of life
—God, your heavenly Father.

Steps

Each of us has a path in life.
Some may walk, some may run,
and others may crawl.
Our directions, we will choose.
—a privilege, given by the Creator.
Some will understand, some will play,
yet others will have it only their way.
Each day and night, another step and direction
is taken with or without thought.
Some steps are taken in the Light
while others are taken in the Dark.
In the Light, all things are seen
—the truth, our surroundings, our path.
In Darkness, all is hidden, nothing revealed.
Some will take their chance, some will fall,
and others will make steps
blind and without direction,
going only deeper into the Dark.
Without the Light freely given to man,
in darkness he will always stand.
With the Light, all is made known,
so step into it and look to your heart
for there is the source,
your direction and life.
Step closer to the Light,
to where it shines the brightest.

Your Breath

Dust blowing
in the winds of time
shadows man with each footstep,
leaving words of eternity
mingling before us all.

Dust to clay in a day;
man's dust at His feet.
The Light of God glorifies it,
tears of mercy mold the clay,
and eternal life pours from His Holy Spirit
onto those who believe
I am that I am.

Splinters of wood pierced His body,
but there's glory in it all.
Hear His voice
and listen to your heartbeat
—your breath of life
in the winds of time.

His Voice

Love Me as I love you.
Bring Me your pain; I have carried your cross.
My life I gave freely for all eternity.
Forever, I will be with you:
sea-to-sea, the air you breathe,
from mountains to valleys, come to Me.
There, I will be with My Father.

Hear My words; I am reaching out to you.
Allow Me into your hearts and receive the glory;
you will see My grace
and your soul will be set free.
All of this awaits; clear your mind
and search for words
to be heard
deep inside you.

Willing

Willing to love the Son as the Father;
living your faith without yesterdays or tomorrows
amongst the heavens and all known,
awaiting wisdom.

Are you willing?

Faith is in your heart.

Without End

Have a Valentine's dream
not far from winding creeks
where orange and yellow butterflies
dance with falling leaves.

Hear sounds of a waterfall
as robins and bluebirds sing
and the colors of a hummingbird appear;
feel the warmth of a boulder
in a cool mountain stream
where rainbow trout swim.

The smell of the forest clings;
a carpet of moss and fern, deep and green,
points to where deer roam
wild and free like the summer breeze
crossing a horizon of red and gold sunsets
—a Valentine's dream without end.

Touching Life

Rainbows in the valley below
stand in the path of dreams;
there flows a wonder mostly unseen,
framed by rugged cliffs
and sky with hints of green.

Eyes of beauty call
as gusts of wind beyond each turn
sail off to the heavens
—the breath of God
living in the rainbow,
touching life.

Tears of Salvation

There was a time when I was lost and without glory.
Then I could not see the life planned for me,
but now I look back and know why my mother said,
"Yesterday, I cried tears of a sinner.
Today, I cry tears of Salvation."

The Lord is showing you the way;
let no man lead you astray,
for now is your day of salvation.
Rejoice in the name of the Lord;
the time is at hand.
Listen to your faith; the words are there.
He asks only that you believe in Him,
then know the Glory you bring to Him.

He will let you see tears of salvation.

Ever Wondered?

Ever wondered why leaves change color,
why a baby's face brings a tear,
or why a clear sky washes away blues?
Clouds in the right place
put your heart in *its* place.
Hear whispering love, saying:

All this and more I created for you
so that you may see My wonder
and hear My words.

Color of the leaves, tears in your eyes,
and the summer's breeze,
—know from whence and why these came;
not by accident, but created for man
to see that all has been planned.

Now you understand how and why,
so let your spirit flow; be a wonder,
a new color, a tear of joy, and a spiritual breeze.
He is why you wondered
and why you now comprehend.

At Twilight

I awaken.
The full moon
gleams behind treetops.

Across mountain peaks
distant fog drifts
with falling leaves
that change color
as a cool breeze
twirls them.

I make my bed
near a flickering fire
and stretch my arms
to the wonderous sky,
casting shadows
on the mountain.

At twilight, I dream
of memories
and old desires.

Unbounded Love

As sure as stars twinkle in the night;
the sun rises in morning light,
and dawn turns crystalline frost to dew,
a rose's beauty smells of sweet nectar
and marks my coming for you.

Days of dreams follow,
touching your heart with sunbeams.
Though apart
we are one
forever
in unbounded love.

Blue-Eyed Tears

A time-creased face lives
with the glow of honey and roses,
eyes of blue wonder
guided by the living light of love
in her last days.

She smiles to the heavens
and touches our hearts
as tears flow
down her cheeks.

Thank God,

again we see living tracks
of blue-eyed tears
for the last time.

To Comprehend

Stir with wonder for an early morning sunrise
—the glare through trees, rustling leaves.
Cool air lifts light mist
into blue sky.
Listen to birdsongs;
breathe deeply
and remember why
it's all here for you.

There is No Excuse

Words of Mine I left you, forever;
I touched your soul, forever;
My only Son bled and died for you, forever.
Given to you by faith,
you are saved;
living forever in the Spirit of God,
the Creator of all generations and time.

All has been revealed;
I have poured out My Holy Spirit
in remembrance of the saints.
Your nature reveals all.
Your heart tells all.
You are Joy in Me, your God.

You see Me and you see the Father.
From the cross I arose.
There is no excuse.
My words speak to you.
All My saints I will call to Glory
as heavenly trumpets sound.

Lift Me up; renew your hearts and soul.
The Glory of God has spoken:
I am that I am—your faith, your life.
Your heart speaks to Me,
and you hear Me in your heart.
Stand still and listen;
I am speaking.

Call on the saints to rejoice in My name.
On the cross, I felt your pains
and remembered each.
My life I did give.
I am that I am,
today and forever.

That, you can see.

The Joy of a Day

You answered our thirst and hunger.
Today, You will touch our hearts again.
Meeting faces, new and old,
with songs of victory, rejoicing with our Lord.
May we glorify Your name.

Thank You Lord, for loving me,
for remembering my valleys and mountain tops,
and offering glory, resurrection,
and peace in the joy of a day.

To Keep

With vision,
an understanding of life grows;
our needs we broadcast
in sunny or stormy weather,
seeking both the end of plans
and understanding.

Seen, heard, touched
and found in eyes of blue,
these words placed here to do just that
touched you.

Today

In another place and time
dreams are reality and life is a dream.
In day, light touches darkness;
darkness becomes the light of men's dreams.

Into the unknown lands of a new world—
each step measured by courage
and strength of will
—take another step closer to destiny.

Sleeping in your dreams,
awaken today to take yet another step
until you find reality again.

Words of Destiny

I write words today
in hopes for tomorrow
and to bring Light out of Darkness.

Lay before me, all to see,
in the Light
that shadows follow
along life's path;
be my guiding hand
in this timeless journey.

Stand still and listen
to words of destiny
in the heavens,
beyond the stars.